*VISITOR'S GUIDE*

# THE CATHEDRAL
# OF
# SEVILLE

Juan Guillén Torralba

© ALDEASA ® : 1996

Depósito Legal: M-14957-1995

I.S.B.N.:84-8003-048-8

**Design and Layout:** Juan Manuel Domínguez

**General Coordinator:** Ángeles Martín

**Translation**: Alicia L. Amatriain

**Photographs:** Covadonga de Noriega

**Photomechanical:** Lucam

**Cover illustration:** Print of Matías de Arteaga, 1671

**Printed in Spain by:** Julio Soto, Impresor, S. A. Madrid

(Printed in Spain)

# INDEX

Aerial view of the Cathedral.

**L**et us build such a large church that those who may eventually see it finished will consider that we are crazy.

The cathedral of Seville, a work imagined by lunatics and carried out by Titans, is a temple for the adorer, a museum for the artist, an archive for the researcher and a library for the curious. Pictures and sculptures, gold work and fabrics, documents and books, constitute a first-rate artistic-documentary complex. Being a successful amalgamation of Christianity and Islam, it contains a unique series of jewels from the Gothic and the Renaissance periods, from the Plateresque and the Baroque in a one-and-only symphony. The Cathedral, along with the Giralda, is the synthesis of Seville, its poster and its lure.

The Giralda through pinnacles.

### THE ENVIRONMENT

Quarter A. District 1. Block 13, it is identified in this way by a slab on its main façade. The Cathedral - church and annexes - forms an enormous free-standing block, limited by the steps and the 157 linked columns, in line with the floor plan of the large Mosque, although its Christian conquerors tried to surpass it. The temple measures in the inside, from east to west: 130,90 mts. and outside 140,50 mts; from the north to the south 140,70 and 161,30 mts. More than 14,500 square mts. in all. It is made up by five longitudinal naves and nine transverse naves, plus two more naves that constitute the chapels. Its width ranges between 10-16 mts. Seventy ogival vaults roof it which are supported by the walls of the chapels and by thirty two free-standing and octagonal pillars. The mosque had seventeen naves of eleven sections and about one hundred sixty pillars. The heights are very proportionate: the central nave and the transept measure 35,5 mts., the vault 39 mts, the aisles 24 mts and the chapels 12,75 mts. The resulting structure is, like the Mosque used to be, a rectangle; it is considered as the most northerly of Spain inasmuch as its head is flat and the arms of the transept hardly jut out which, along with the central nave, simulate a latin cross of the kind of a *hallenkirche cathedral*, characteristic of the German Gothic style. The block where the Cathedral stands, with the annexes that complete it, measures 173,05 x 148,80 mts. and its area reaches 23,475 square mts. It is the largest Gothic Cathedral and the third church in the world, only surpassed by St. Peter's in Rome and St. Paul's in London. It appears in the *Guinnes Book of Records* as the largest world's area with 126,18 mts long, 82,60 wide and 30,48 high. UNESCO proclaimed it as Patrimony of the Humanity in 1987. The Magna Hispalensis, the Nobilis Burgensis (Burgos), the Pulchra Leonina (León) and the Dives Toletana (Toledo) sublimate the Gothic in Spain.


### THE HISTORY

The Cathedral of Seville is settled over the large Almohad mosque built by the caliph Abu Yacub Yusuf's initiative (1172-1182); rests of the mosque can be seen in the Patio de los Naranjos (Orange trees courtyard) and in some of the **external doors**, two of which are still being used: the **Perdón** (Forgiveness) and del **Lagarto** (Lizard) doors. After the Reconquer of Spain the mosque was consecrate as cathedral and adsapted to the Christian worship (December 1243). It remained in such way until July 8, 1401 when, being Seville without an archbishop, the canons made a decision as crazy and sublime that only the Sevillian hot summer weather could inspire:

**Whereas the Church was vacant (...) while the Dean, the Canons, the Dignitaries, the Prebendaries and companions were present, they stated, that since the Church of Seville threatened every day to collapse (...), therefore another such a Church being so good that it will not been excelled by any**

other similar would exist and that the grandness and author-ity of Seville and its Church be considered as the reason gov-erns; and should not the income be enough for such purpose, all the attendants agreed to take from their own income an amount enough, that they shall give it in behalf of God's service; and they ordered to two Canons to sign it.

The people summed up this decision and according to one of them: **Let us build such a large church that those who may eventually see it finished will consider that we are crazy.** Said

Door of the Baptistery.

Door of St. Michael or of The Epiphany.

canons honoured their pledge and almost saw it finished. The work began in 1408, and in hardly seventy years the cathedral was a fact. In spite of the fact that it is the work of many people, it shows a great unity: the idea prevailed over the time. It is not known who designed it; out of the architects of the beginning we know Alonso Martínez and Pedro García, foreigners such as Isambret, Carlín and Juan Norman; Juan de Hoces was main master from 1478 to 1496, Simón of Cologne may have built the dome (incidentally, the one he built in the Burgos Cathedral fell down, 1495-1498); some others attribute it to Alonso Rodríguez (1496-1513). Juan Gil de Hontañón (1513-1519) finished

the Gothic work, the last stone was placed on October 10, 1506 and on March 11, 1507 it was considered to be finished. The dome collapsed in December 1511 and its reconstruction gave rise to the Renaissance remodelling. Distinguished masters such as Diego de Riaño (1528-1534), Martín de Gaínza (1534-1556), Hernán Ruíz el Mozo (1557-1569), Pedro Díaz Palacios (1569-1574), Juan de Maeda (1574-1576) and Asensio de Maeda (1576-1602) worked on it: the fruits of these inspirations proclaim their mastery.

### EXTERIORS

**Main Façade**. It faces the Avenida de la Constitución, the most cosmopolitan road of Seville. It insinuates the inner structure of five naves and side chapels, and allows to see easily the flying buttress that support them. Three doors are in this side: San Miguel, La Asunción and Bautisterio. The oldest are the lateral ones (master Carlín, XVth century). The relief of *The Birth* in the one of **San Miguel,** The Baptism of Jesus in the **Bautisterio** door and *The Assumption* in the central door embellish their **tympanums.** The **sculptures** of the oldest (Mercadante de Bretaña and Pedro Millán XVth century)) are made of baked clay, keeping in mind that Seville is land of potters; they were polychrome lighting with their colour the doors, which are nowadays monochrome. The **main door** is not inferior of the whole despite the fact that it was carried out in the XIXth century (design of Fernando Rosales and decoration of Ricardo Bellver). The Sagrario Church, which construction began in 1618, follows the Gothic fabric.

**Façade of the Alemanes Street**. The crenellated wall with lower buttresses betrays its Almohad origin; the **door of the For-**

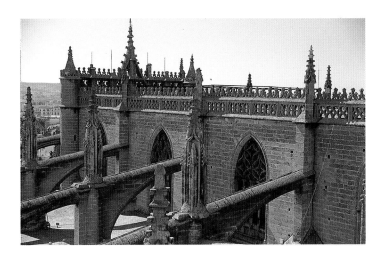

Buttresses of the Cathedral.

Door of the Assumption.

**giveness** is also from the same origin, it is the most important access to the **sahn** or **Courtyard of the Ablutions,** that faced the main entrance to the Mosque, looking from North to South. This door, although retouched, keeps its Islamic charm; the two leaves of cedar wood, covered with bronze, are the original ones, they measure 9 x 2 mts. and are decorated with vegetal motifs and Arabic words; the doorknockers are reproductions of the originals that are exhibited at the Cathedral, they are shaped like

Christ of the Forgiveness.

the Almohad palm that seems to be embroidered in bronze with inscriptions from the Koran. All the metal was chiselled by hand. On both sides of the door two large terracotta **sculptures**: *St. Peter and St. Paul,* and two others representing an Annunciation: *Angel and Mary;* and a **relief**, *The Expulsion of the Merchants* (Miguel Florentín, 1519-1522). There is a small **altarpiece** in the hall with an Ecce Homo, The Christ of the Forgiveness (XVIIIth century), that named the door. At the corner with Placentines is the **door of the Columbus Library**. Cervantes placed in these steps *Rinconete and Cortadillo* scenes: Monopodio had his academy not far away from here.

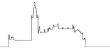

**Façade of the Front.** The Almohad fabric that ends in the **Lizard door** follows from the corner to the tower. The Giralda acts like a bridge between the Moslem and the Gothic. The front part is limited by two of the most intimate squares of Seville for their Marian dedication: Virgin of the Reyes and Triunfo (Immaculate). This façade has two **Gothic doors**: the one of the Los **Palos** which **tympanum** encloses an *Epiphany* where the beautiful face of the Virgin stands out; then the door of the **Campanilla,** showing *Christ's Entry into Jerusalem;* these reliefs are framed by prophets and saints of baked clay (M. Florentín, XVIth century). The **apse** of the **Royal Chapel** highlights among the doors (1520-1523).

**Southern Façade.** The Church elbows with the Palace of the Regional Government, with the aristocracy of the Alcázar: walls, door of the Lion and the arch of the entrance to the Flags court-

Western Façade.

Door of the Palos.

Door of La Campanilla.

Christ's Entry into Jerusalem, Tympanum of the Door of La Campanilla.

yard; and with the elegance of the Lonja, nowadays Archivo de Indias, by Juan Herrera, a Sevillian version of the Escorial, and the Immaculate's monument in the middle. From here, looking at the Cathedral, one's eyes inundate with the beauty of a forest of flying buttresses, pinnacles, balustrades that enhance even more the grandeur and the symmetry of the fabric; certainly it is one of the most classic and suggestive places in the world, as stated by the Emperor Carlos V. The **door of St. Christopher** or *the Prince* is the only one at this side, it was the King's entrance due to its proximity to the Alcazar. It is retracted by the building of the Renaissance area. The design of the door was from Demetrio Ríos and it was performed under the direction of Alfonso Fernández Casanova (1887-1895).

**The Cathedral of Seville, an enormous fortress of the Catholic faith, settles it bells in the Moslem Giralda and**

Door of The Prince.

Exterior of the Patio de los Naranjos, Sahn of the Mosque.

**keeps, in the depths of itself, its Arabian Patio de los Naranjos. (Marguerite Yourcenar).**

### THE PATIO DE LOS NARANJOS

An oasis of peace in the very heart of the city, it shows from the entrance its Almohad kindred: the door, the rests of the Mosque pillars, the enclosure, the corridor of the nave of the Lizard with double slope, the font for the ablutions (although its origin is Roman). From the door of the Lizard to that of the Forgiveness, the Archive of the Cathedral and the **Chapter and Columbus libraries** are located, pride and worry of the Chapter. The **Chapel of la Granada** in which some Visigothic Capitals are kept is next to

View of the Patio de los
Naranjos from The Giralda.

the door. The patio has very peculiar reminiscences: In October 1498, Antonio de Nebrija asked for the license to teach grammar in the Chapel of the Granada; the Chapter ordered "that whatever should be made necessary to deck with benches and mats". The venerable Contreras, St. Vincent Ferrer, St. Francis Borgia preached, among others, in the small pulpit leant to the nave. The famous *Lagarto* (lizard), an elephant tusk, a stick and a brake hang in the corridor; presents, votive offerings, so what?; the **painting** of the *Cristo de los Escobones* (Christ of the large brooms) on the wall, called in this way as his lamp was supported thanks to the money obtained from the discarded brooms. All of this does transform it into an evocative place: the symmetry of the orange trees, the interior of the Almohad doors, the view of the Giralda which from this patio seems even higher, remembrances of Nebrija's sermons and lectures, of sweepers that try to keep alight an oil lamp at the feet of a Crucified.

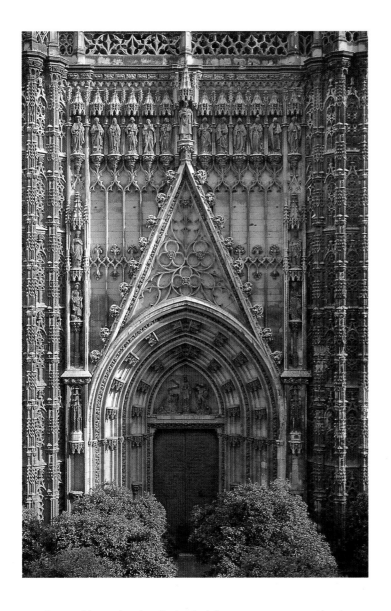

Door of The Conception.

From this patio the Cathedral has two accesses: the huge **door of The Conception** (Adolfo Fernádez Casanova, 1895-1927) that imitates old models: in the **tympanum** of the *Immaculate, St. Miachael* and *St. John Evangelist* and above *Jesus and His Apostles*. The sculptures are by Joaquín Bilbao, Adolfo

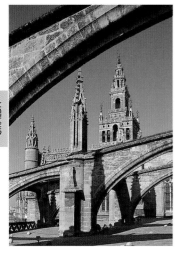

The Giralda is silhouetted against the architecture of the Cathedral.

The Giralda. Central section.

The Giralda. Detail of the central section.

López and Eduardo Muñoz. At the other **door,** the one of Granada, simple and noble, *The Virgin of el Reposo (Rest) with David and Solomon* (Mercadante or by Pedro Millán, XVth century) welcome the traveller.

### THE GIRALDA

**"The Tower sleeps standing
and the Cathedral does it lying,
that the Giralda is life
and the Cathedral Faith.
From the square one can see
the bells flying
the Prayers waiting.
And by themselves, without bell-ringer
they move their steel tongues
and  St. Ferdinand awakes.
(Fernando Villalón)**

Versatile metaphor: Islamic minaret conceived in stone and finished in brick, **Turris fortissima** from the Proverbs Book (chap. 18, v. 10), converted into Christian, Faith pedestal and symbol of the city.

Apse of the Royal
Chapel with the Giralda
in the background.

When the Mosque was hardly finished, Ben Basso began to
build the tower (1184) and the Almohad victory over Alfonso VIII
(Alarcos, 1195) accelerated its completion (Alí de Gomara, 1198). A
group of four golden bells topped it: yamur. The earthquake in
August 24, 1356 knocked it down, giving raise to its remodelling,
brilliantly carried out by Hernán Ruíz el Mozo (1558-1568);  the
Giraldillo was forged simultaneously (1565-1568). According to

The Cathedral.

Nightfall.

Inside the Cathedral: different volumes.

investigations made in 1987 this huge tower has only a few meters of foundation.

The tower measures 93,90 mts. and it is arranged in the exterior in three vertical panels: one of windows and two diamond shape decorated lateral ones of engraved bricks. The way up is a very smooth ramp until the belfry; from here on, it is by steps. The **Renaissance belfry** is formed by the group of Bells with four pots of lilies, adorned with head reliefs; that of the Reloj (Clock), in which frieze it is stated: TURRIS-FORTISSIMA-NOMEN DÑI-PROV.18, with some more reliefs; the group of the *Estrellas* (Stars), with faces that represent the winds, and that of the *Bolas* (Balls) over which a *dome* and the pedestal of the *Giraldillo*. A replica of it is exhibited in the Cathedral.

### INSIDE THE CATHEDRAL

**"Everything is severe and majestic, like if we had left the real world and we were in an immense cavern, prepared by a giant in love with the geometry, symmetry and order." (Fernando Chueca Goitia).**

The visitor has a feeling of smallness in the presence of the greatness, and of quietness before the penumbra. Silence prevails. Light trembles and creates that special atmosphere that fascinated

the romantics. Eighty one stained-glass windows sieve and make iridescent the luminosity of Seville, perhaps the most interesting and complete group of Spain. Works of artists such as Arnao de Vergara, Arnao de Flandes, Carlos de Brujas, Vicente Menardo, Jean Jacques (XVth-XVIth century and some modern ones).

Transept, stone embroidery.

Light spreads out: detail.

The shadow stands out the illuminated architecture.

21

The Virgin of El Pilar.

St. Jude, a very special devotion.

## NORTHERN CHAPELS

**Chapel of El Pilar.** It already existed in the former Mosque-Cathedral; it had been founded by Aragonese nobles. The **image** of The *Virgin of El Pilar*, of polychrome terracotta, might be the most successful work of Pedro Millán (1500). Of elegant shape, it emanates nobility and elegancy, dignity and mysticism. The Child smiles and blesses. An image of *St. Jude*, in the altar on the right side, has made this chapel very popular lately.

Above this chapel, a beautiful **stained-glass window** (1) of Arnao de Flandes: *Christ entering into Jerusalem.*

**Chapel of the Evangelists**. There is beauty in everything: in the inner **glass-stained window** (2), *The Birth* (Arnao de Flandes, 1553); and in the nine **paintings** on wood by Hernando de Esturmio (XVIth century): in the middle *St. Gregory's Mass,* above it *The Resurrection,* on the sides, *The Evangelists;* above the altar of *St. Catherine* and *St. Barbara; St. Sebastian, St. John the Baptist and St. Antón;* and *the Saints Justa and Rufina with the Giralda* as it was before the refurbishing by Hernán Ruíz. The purity and perfection of the drawing are remarkable as well as the colour. Some of the pieces used in the choir that is erected on Holy Thursday and on Corpus Christi day are exhibited: large lecterns for the choral books, stretchers to carry the candles, etc., of golden and polychrome woodcut with floral ornaments and child angels. (XVIIIth century).

*The Lazarus resurrection,* Arnao de Flandes' (1554) (3) **stained-glass window** is placed above the gate.

**Chapel of the Annunciation. The stained-glass window** (4) fuses the *Annunciation with the Virgin who protects the maidens* (A. de Vergara, 1534). It so happens that a foundation (XVIth century) dedicated to provide dowries for marriageable maidens was situated there; the *Annunciation* can be seen again in the altarpiece (José Rivera, 1771). Actually, the main jewels are the **paintings** on wood of the original reredos (Cristobal de Morales, XV-XVIth century): Delivery of the Dowry, the Donor and his coat of arms; *St. Jerome and St. Gregory, St. Bartholomew, St. Peter, St. Thomas and St. James the Less, St. Ambrose and St. Agustin, and a Calvary; the Saviour* that we find in the centre was carried out later on. It has two iron screens, both are remarkable; the lateral one ends in the *Annunciation* of embossed iron.

**A stained-glass window** (5) by A. de Vergara, *Mary Magdalene washing Christ's feet* (1554), is above the chapel.

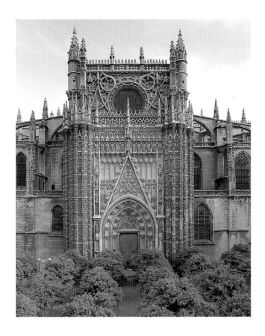

Door of The Conception in the green of the orange trees.

Elements of the portable organ.

**Door of the Conception.** *The Allegory of the Immaculate Conception Dogma with Sevillian environment* (Alfonso Grosso, 1966) is below the rose window. On the sides there are two symmetrical altars: one with the *Assumption of the Virgin* (Gregorio Ferrari, XVIIIth century). On the left side shines the *Virgin of Bethlehem,* one of the most beautiful paintings of Alonso Cano (1635); above, the *Holy Trinity* (Virgilio Mattoni, 1901). On the left-hand wall *The Killing of the Holy Innocents,* perhaps of Jacopo Fardella (XVIIth century).

Imposition of the chasuble to St.Ildefonse, by Valdés Leal.

**The stained-glass windows** of this room can be seen from here: The Assumption over the door (6); *The Resurrection* (7) (Carlos de Brujas, 1558) on the gaps; several *Apostles and Saints* (8) carried out by Arnao de Flandes between 1543-1551.

**Chapel of St. Francis.** The poor Saint from Assisi is praised by the magnificent **stained-glass window** (9) with *The Ecstasy* (Arnao de Flandes, 1554) and in the altarpiece (Bernardo Simón de Pineda, 1661) the splendid canvas with *The Apotheosis* (1656), "one of the best works of Francisco de Herrera el Mozo, according to the fancy composition, soft colour, red and transparent inks and the good contrast of the light and the dark

Sepulchre of Archbishop Gonzalo de Mena: Chapel of St. James.

with which it is painted" (Ceán Bermúdez). *The Imposition of the Chasuble upon St. Ildefonsus* (Valdés Leal, 1661) with excellent realism and composition is above it. A small altarpiece with *St. Teresa* (XVIIth century), a bust of an Ecce Homo and some pictures complete the room.

**The stained-glass window** (10) exalts *St. Francis surrounded by some saints of his Order* (E. Alemán, 1478).

**Chapel of St. James the Apostle.** It is a small and heterogeneous museum: a splendid iron screen, **stained-glass window** (11) that depicts *The Conversion of St. Paul* (Menardo, 1560) and an impressive altarpiece ornamented with angels and vegetal motifs (B.S. de Pineda, 1663), and the monumental canvas *St. James in the Battle of Clavijo* (Juan de Roelas) and above it, *The Martyrdom of St. Lawrence* (Valdés Leal, 1663). A Pietá (Sevillian School, XVIth century) is venerated on the altar top. A collection of fifteen paintings on wood that come from the former altarpiece reliquary of the Main Sacristy (Antón Pérez, 1547-1548) is exhibited in this area.

Virgin of The Cushing.

Even more: two **sculptural jewels**, as different as beautiful and unique: the splendid *sepulchre of the Archbishop of Seville Don Gonzalo de Mena* (1394-1401), Gothic work of alabaster with reliefs with motifs of the Gospel on its front and sides, including the one leant against the wall; the figure of the archbishop lies on top of the sarcophagus. The other is a relief of glazed terracotta: The Virgin of the Cushion. The Child sat on a cushion plays with Mary's veil and His Mother caresses His naked foot. (Andrea della Robbia's workshop, XV-XVIth century). The beauty of Mary, the Child's expression, the composition and the softness of colours stand out.

Mausoleum of Bishop Don Baltasar del Río: Chapel of Scalas.

Virgin of The Granada.

Chapel of Scalas.

**A stained-glass window** with *St. Justa and Rufina* (12), *St. James and St. Barbara* (13) (E. Alemán) is above the chapel.

**Chapel of Scalas**. Beautiful Renaissance iron screen with *the Virgin and the Apostles* made of corrugated iron sheet (1564), **stained-glass window** (14), depicting *The Coming of the Holy Spirit and two Canons* (1880) and the monumental marble *sepulchre of Don Baltasar del Río*, archdeacon and canon of Niebla, bishop of Scalas, and relative of Julio the IInd and León the Xth. It is composed of a catafalque with the reclining statue of the founder, held by two little angels with corbels adorned with a beautiful medallion with a relief of The Virgin of the Consolación in the background, and St. Peter and St. Paul at the sides. The majestic **altarpiece** is erected above the tribune, and it is divided in three vertical sections by two plateresque columns in which pedestals appear the bishop and his coat of arms. Over the altar, in bas-relief, *The Miracle of the Loaves and the Fishes* and above *The Coming of the Holy Spirit* with a remarkable composition and treatment of the figures; a **bust** of *The Heavenly Father worshipped by two angels*

crowns it. This mausoleum is empty: the bishop died and was buried in Rome. The monument is of Italian style and dates from May 5, 1539. This chapel had an exit to the Patio de los Naranjos; its front, that still exists, was designed by Hernán Ruíz or by Pedro de Riaño.

Across the monumental jewel, a work of art: *The Virgin of the Granada,* a superb **terracotta** work of Lucca della Robbia: the Virgin, surrounded by saints and crowned by angels, offers a pomegranate to Her Child (XIV-XVth century).

Above the chapel, a **stained-glass window** (15) of E. Alemán (1478): *Four Apostles.*

**Chapel of St. Anthony or Baptistery. A stained-glass window** (16) depicting *Sts. Justa and Rufina and the Incumbent* (Juan Bautista de León, 1685) illuminates this chapel. From the transversal nave it seems as if the Renaissance font, with angels on its base and vegetal motifs in the basin, were holding the large frame (Pineda, 1668) with two outstanding Murillo works : *St. Anthony* (1566) and *The Baptism of Christ* (1668). The former, in spite of its large dimensions (5,60 x 3,75), exudes intimacy: the Saint, entranced, sees how heaven opens and, Child Jesus, among angels, descends. A monk table in the forefront and a cloister in the background enlivens the scene. The simplicity and tenderness of the subject, the play of light and half-light, make of this painting one of the most appreciated pictures of this painter. The other painting of Murillo, allusive to the sacramental function of the chapel, is of a similar beauty.

Baptismal font: Chapel of St. Anthony.

Stained-glass window of St. Justa and St. Rufina.

Stained-glass window with four apostles, transept .

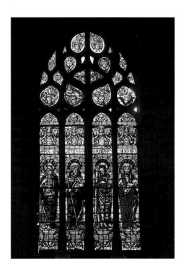

A **beam** of eighteen woods with *Apostles, Prophets and Saints and the Pietá* (XVIth century), completes the beauty of this place. A perfect restoration job has given back to the faces the firmness and clarity in its lines and its original colour. Other important works: The Immaculate (Roelas), *St. Peter praying before Christ and St. Peter in Prison* (Valdés Leal) and two pictures about *The Creation* (Simón de Vos).

**A stained-glass window** (17) by E. Alemán: *The Four Evangelists* (1478) is above the chapel.

**Door of the Shrine.** Opened up in 1682 and adorned with statues of the Patron Saints: *St. Ferdinand, Leandro and St. Isidoro, Sts. Justa and Rufina*, serves as backcloth to the reproduction of The Giraldillo, name of the weather-vane that crowns the belfry: a woman symbolizes the Catholic Church triumphant over the heresy and the Turks, an idea of the canon and humanist Francisco Pacheco. Bartolomé Morel casted it between 1566 and 1568 (August 13). It measures 7,52 meters from the ball base to the cross.

## WESTERN CHAPELS

**Chapel of las Angustias.** Juan de Roelas' **painting** (1609): Mary receives Her inert Son, over a dark background, Mary Magdalene and St. John accompany Her. Angels with symbols of The Passion hold the solomonic columns of the altarpiece and, at the top, *the Holy Face between Faith and Hope.*

**Altar of the Visitation**. Incomparable collection of **paintings** on wood of Pedro de Villegas Marmolejo, a great Sevillian painter; his signature can be seen in the central painting, *The Visitation of Mary to St. Elizabeth*; it is accompanied by *St. Blas, The Baptism of Christ, St. James and St. Sebastian* above the altar portraits of the donor and his family, in the middle *Jesus Child full of glory* (1566). The accuracy of the drawing, the nobility of the forms and the soft and fresh colour stand out. Above the altar there is a high-relief of St. Jerome Penitent (Jerónimo Hernández, 1566), a very much achieved work due to its naturalism in the design and the modelling of the anatomy. The iron screen dates from 1568.

Above the Baptistery door, *The Visitation* a Renaissance **stained-glass window (**18) of Vicente Menardo (1568).

**Altar of the Virgin of the Escobilla.** The *Pietá* group, of baked and polychrome **terracotta**, with Flemish influences. (XIVth century).

Dumb Child.

**Chapel of St. Leandro**. It has a portal of profusely carved stone, Baroque iron screen and the altarpiece with solomonic columns (1730); *St. Leandro, St. Fulgencio and St. Antón* are in the centre and *St. Domingo* at the top (Duque Cornejo, 1734); and two canvases with events of the Saint's life. (J. Mausola, 1735).

**Altar of the Christ Child.** This delightful **image**, of polychromatic wood, Martínez Montañés' school (XVIth century), also known as *El Niño Mudo* (The Mute Child) because of the shape of His lips, has been and still is subject to a great popular devotion.

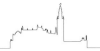

Virgin of The Madrona.

Virgin of The Cinta.

**Altar of the Consolation**. *The Virgin with The Child between St. James the Greater* and *St. Anthony* is in its centre, painted over a Gothic panel (Alonso M. de Tovar 1720); at its foot the Donor.

**Stained-glass windows**: Rose window (19) (2,8 mts. diameter) with *The Evangelists* (20) (V. Menardo, 1566); in the nave, *Dignitaries of the Bible* (21) (E. Alemán, 1478-1483).

Between the retrochoir and the portal, Don Hernando Columbus, son of the Discoverer of America, one of the greatest bibliophiles of the world who donated his Library to the Cathedral is buried; he died in July of 1539.

Above the main door there is a **Calvary, a sculptural group,** work of Francisco Antonio Girón. It crowned the great monument of Maundy Thursday.

**Altar de Plata.** Leant against the interior of the main portal, the great silver altar is raised from Maundy Thursday until the Corpus Christi feast; it is a work of Juan de Laureano Pina and Mateo Gutiérrez (1688-1690). It includes numerous busts and saint statues and is topped by a large sun and a crown; the urn that houses the gold Chalice where the Eucharist is kept, is placed in the centre.

**Altar of the Guardian Angel.** One of the most evocative works of Murillo (1665) interprets the idea of the Angel that assists the man, always a child.

**Altar of the Virgin of the Madrona.** An intimate scene: the Mother offers her naked breast to the Child who looks at the watcher; a kneeling angel offers a basket with strawberry-like berries. An **alabaster group** by Lorenzo Mercadante de Bretaña (XVth century). It is 1,20 mts high and it is really admirable because of its modelling, the expressions of the faces and the set of the robes; at the top of the altarpiece *The Scourging of Jesus.*

**Chapel of St. Isidoro**. It matches with the one of St. Leandro; the portal in profusely carved stone, a beautiful iron gate (XVIIth century) and the inside of polychrome plaster. The altarpiece with solomonic columns (B. Simón de Pineda, 1662-1664) frames four anonymous images: *St. Isidoro, accompanied by St. Francis and St. Diego de Alcalá and* at the attic, *St. Ferdinand.*

**Altar of the Virgin of la Cinta**. Another of Mercadante de Bretaña's jewel, of baked and polychrome **terracotta**; a full-size Virgin with Her Son in Her arms. The features are very expressive, the cloak is held by the Virgin and the robe is gracefully fastened with a girdle; The Child holds a book in His hands. It dates from between 1460-1470.

Chapel of St. Isidoro.

Altarpiece of the Chapel of St. Laureano.

Above the door of St. Michael there is a Renaissance **stained-glass window** (22) with *The Annunciation* by V. Menardo (1566).

**Altar of the Birth.** Behind a Plateresque iron screen (XVIth century), an altarpiece with paintings by Luís de Vargas can be admired; Francisco Pacheco called him: " The light of painting and its praiseworthy father, in Seville his home town". *The Adoration of the Shepherds is in the centre, and on the sides: The Annunciation, The Presentation, St. John, St. Luke, St. Matthew, St. Mark and the Epiphany.*

## SOUTHERN CHAPELS

**Chapel of St. Laureano.** According to tradition this Saint was the archbishop of Seville: the **stained-glass window** (23) in which *St. Laureano, St. Isidoro* and *St. Leandro* (Vicente  Menardo 1572) appear, proves it.  Although it is true what Ceán Bermúdez said

Sepulchre of Cardinal
de la Lastra.

SOUTHERN
CHAPELS

Christ of Maracaibo.

about it: "The foundation stone of the Cathedral was placed in this chapel when the construction of the Cathedral started and, since it was the first to be finished, the Divine Offices were held there until the Cathedral was completed", everything inside dates back to the XVIIIth century. The **altarpiece** depicts the *Titular* Saint and scenes of his life; above a relief of his *Martyrdom* and angels with fringes. *The pictures with scenes of the Saint's life* are of the Sevillian Matías de Arteaga (1700-1702). Frames, altarpiece and figures are from an anonymous artist. The chapel was used as a burial place for different dignitaries, but the *Mausoleum of Cardinal Don Joaquín Lluch y Garriga* (1877-1882) is the only one that is visible: over a podium ornamented with angels and coats of arms is the Archbishop in a praying position (Agapito Vallmitjana, 1885). Above the chapel, there is a **stained-glass window** (24) of E. Alemán with several *Saints*.

**Chapel of the Maracaibo Christ.** *The Holy Family* (1798) is a **stained-glass window** (25) of the interior of the chapel. Facing it, there is an **altarpiece** of Joaquín Bilbao (1914) with a *Crucified Christ*, a beautiful painting that belonged to some of the original chapels (XVIth century); modern **bas-reliefs** depicting the *Virgin and St. John* are at the sides. **Said painting** is venerated as The Holy Christ of Maracaibo. On the left side wall, on a tribune with a balustrade, an **altarpiece** (XVth century) with paintings on wood shines: *St. Bartholomew with St. Blas and St. Nicholas, St. James and St. Sebastian* at its sides; above this section a **sculpture** of *The Virgin*

Altarpiece of the Chapel of St. Joseph.

with *Child* (XVIth century), flanked by *St. John the Baptist, St. Ann, St. Martha and St. Michael*; five pictures of *The Passion* are in the lower part of the predella and a *Crucifixion* in the centre of it. They have been restored recently and thus all their beauty can be appreciated.

The *sepulchre in marble of Cardinal Don Luís de la Lastra and Cuesta* (1862-1876), is on the right-hand side. The prelate, on his knees and with a cape, has the mitre at his foot; angels and coats of arms ornament the corners (Ricardo Bellver, 1880).

The **stained-glass window** (26) that is above this chapel depicts *Four Female Saints*. (E. Alemán, 1478).

**Chapel of St. Joseph**. Inside the chapel is *The Nativity* (27) a modern **stained-glass window** (1932). The Neo-Classical marble

St. James the Less.

**altarpiece** (XVIIIth century), shows in its centre the image of the *Incumbent* of polychrome wood (José Esteve Bonet). The *mausoleum and the sarcophagus cover of Cardinal Bueno Monreal* (1954-1982) (Jose Antonio Márquez) are in the front and at the right side the *sepulchre of Cardinal Manuel Joaquín Tarancón y Morón,* archbishop of Seville (1857-1862). Several pictures ornament the interior of the chapel.

A **stained-glass window** (28) depicting the *Saints Gregory Agustín, Ambrosius and Jerome.*

**Chapel of St. Hermenegild**. A **stained-glass window** (29) with the symbols of the *Incumbent* illuminates a simple **altarpiece** with *St. Hermenegild*, of gold-ground and polychrome wood, accompanied by a *Saintly Bishop* and a *Benedictine Female Saint* and *The Virgin of El Carmen* is located at the upper part of it; several angels finish the adornment (Bartolomé García Santiago and son, XVIIIth century). *St. James the Less* can be admired above the altar, he is identifiable by the stick that reminds his death; a magnificent piece of work of Pedro Millán (1506) in which the dignity of his face, the perfection of his hands and the folds arrangement of his robe are really outstanding; it is the only figure that remains after the dome collapsed. The other image of wood (XVIth century) represents *St. James the Greater* in pilgrim clad. Two **busts** of chiselled silver are next to them with reliquaries on their chests and inlaid enamel. They become a part of the silver altar that is set up on Maundy Thursday and Corpus Christi days.

A sublime work of art appears amidst: *Cardinal Juan de Cervantes' sepulchre*, archbishop of Seville (1449-1453) founder of the chapel, a distinguished work of Mercadante de Bretaña. An alabaster tumulus holds the reclining figure of the Cardinal dressed in pontifical; the face corresponds to the death mask; a hind, allusive to the surname of Cervantes, is at his feet. The Mausoleum has four angels with coats of arms at the corners and some other angels and lions on the base. Built between 1453-1458, it connects with the Flemish and Burgundy Renaissance; the angels are reminiscent of Van Eyck.

Above this chapel, a **stained-glass window** (30) of E. Alemán: *Four Saintly Bishops* (1478).

**Chapel of the Virgin of la Antigua. Chapel of the Hispanity or Virgin of the Discovery**, Columbus prayed at Her feet and her devotion extended to the newly discovered lands; this chapel stands out because of its artistic value and its ornamental richness.

The mihrab, a place towards which the Muslims addressed their prayers, was possibly here. Today's chapel is a song to the Virgin of two Sevillian Archbishops: Cardinal Don Diego Hurtado de Mendoza (1495-1502) and Don Luis de Salcedo y Azcona (1722-1741); the architecture is due to the former and the ornamentation to the latter. The Cardinal was very fond of the image that was painted on a wall of the primitive cathedral, so he decided to build a sanctuary for it, converting this chapel into the largest one with a vault that confers it a great distinction. He generously endowed it and that is where he decided to be buried: Alonso Rodríguez (1504) finished the work. The Cardinal foresaw, but he did not see, the relocation of the image next to the wall in the night of November 7-8, 1578. The extremely rich ornamentation was carried out at the expense of Archbishop Salcedo: he commissioned the altarpiece, of marble and jade, to Juan Fernández Iglesias and the sculptures to Pedro Duque Cornejo. The **effigy** of *The Virgin of La Antigua* stands out on its own right, painted in fresco on the wall and it is larger than life-size. Mary has Jesus in Her lap and a rose in Her hand, the Child holds a little bird in His. Three angels stretch out their wings over Her: two of them crown Her and the third one announces a message of hope: Ecce María venit (here comes Mary). They were painted by Antón Pérez (1547). A belittled woman is praying at Her feet. The crowns, made of gold and precious stones, incrusted in the wall, were paid by the people in its Canonical Coronation (1929). The painting, a blend of Gothic and Byzantine, dates from the end of XIVth century and evokes the Siena's Madonnas. The Virgin is framed by **sculptures** of *St. Joachim and St. Ann;* above, *Jesus Saviour with St. John The Baptist and St. John Evangelist*. In the top, two symbolic sculptures and angels in the intermediate frieze. The *tabernacle* is made of chiselled silver (Duque Cornejo) and the *crucifix* of ivory (Cortezo); the frontal part of the altar and the side-table are made of silver, as well as the lectern, the balustrade with the Ave María and the graceful angel that is used for the readings. The two altar doors are carried out in ebony wood with inlaid work of bronze, tortoise shell and ivory. Huge silver lamps illuminate it.

It has two entrances and two fronts. The larger one, with a beautiful wrought-iron screen, was designed by Hernán Ruíz (XVIth-XVIIth century); the one that faces the crossing is a beautiful work of art by Pedro de Riaño although it was finished by Martín de Gainza or Hernán Ruíz. The **figures** of this front carry a teaching: *God Father*, at the top, accompanied by two giants and torches, makes the decision of saving us by means of Jesus: Nativity (upper part); salvation that is made in the Church: *St. Peter and St. Paul,* at

Virgin of La Antigua.

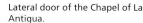

Lateral door of the Chapel of La Antigua.

Reclining statue of Cardinal Hurtado de Mendoza.

the sides over green marble columns, may be originated from the mosque-cathedral and *six Apostles* in the Plateresque arch.

The two Archbishops keep vigil before the Virgin from their **mausoleums**. The one of *Cardinal Hurtado de Mendoza*, with wonderful design and performance, is at the right-hand side of the altar. He is reclining dressed in Pontifical attire under a triumphal arch supported by pillars and six statues: *St. Peter and St. Paul, two Apostles, St. John The Baptist* and a *Saintly Bishop*. A frieze with reliefs can be seen over the sarcophagus, and in panels *The Resurrection* and at their sides *St. Anne with Mary and The Virgin with The Child; The Ascension* in the middle which treatment is very curious: of Jesus, only the feet can be seen and of the Apostles just the back or the profile. Two feminine images and coats of arms accompany the inscription of the catafalque. This marvel of white marble of the famous Domenico A. Fancelli di Settignano (1508-1509) was a decisive fact for the introduction of the Italian Renaissance in Spain.

About *Archbishop Salcedo's sepulchre*, there is not too much to say except that it is an imitation of the aforementioned, performed by Pedro Duque Cornejo (1734-1741). Semicircular arch, next to the columns six statues of saints and above the catafalque Marian scenes in **relief:** *The Annunciation, The Visitation and The Apostles*

beside *The Virgin's Grave*, and crowning it all, *The Assumption*. The finishing is good, but there is no possible comparison with the Cardinal's. The **canvases** that adorn the chapel with topics of The Virgin of La Antigua, among them the transfer of the wall (Domingo Martínez) date also from  Archbishop Salcedo's epoch. Both the fabric and the ornamentation of the chapel, that was very damaged, were restored in 1991-1992. Nowadays it is the Chapel of El Santísimo and is devoted to prayer.

**Altar of the Conception.** A splendid pictorial **altarpiece,** by Luis de Vargas (1561), that symbolizes **The Saviours's  genealogy:** in Jesus, embraced by Mary, culminates the mankind that starts with Adam. The "Leg-Gamba" of Adam, in the foreground, colloquially names this altar. It is said that the Italian Alesio, creator of the huge *St. Christopher* that is  across it, stated "Piú vale la tua gamba che il mio San Cristóforo" (your leg excels my St. Christopher). Likewise, of the same artist are *The Allegory of the Triumphant Church* that is above the altar and at both sides the donor and canon *Don Juan de Medina and his coat of arms.* The wrought iron gate is outstanding: it was designed by Hernán Ruiz and was finished by Pedro Delgado (1562).

**Altar of the Pietá.** Another pictorial **altarpiece** as impressive as the aforementioned. Its author was Alejo Fernández (1527) and it

Virgin of The Olmos.

Altar of The Pietá.

indicates the passing from the Gothic to the Renaissance. The central panel represents *The Virgin with the dead body of Her Son, accompanied by St John, Joseph of Arimathea and The Three Marys*; at the background, quite tenebrist, *Jesus on Abraham's bosom* and *The Appearance to Mary Magdalene;* several Saints at beside. Above, a mascaron belches vegetal motifs. Another panel painting, above the altar, depicts *Jesus tied to the column* and at each side, portraits of the female Donor. The iron screen dates from the XVIth century.

### DOOR OF THE PRINCE

**Monument to Columbus**. Seville and its Cathedral are proud of housing the remains of the discoverer of America, who stayed many years in this city. The remains arrived in 1899 and were buried in this mausoleum in 1902. Four gigantic heralds, of polychrome bronze and alabaster faces, symbolize Castile (it carries Granada in the point of its lance), León, Aragón and Navarra, and they raise to their shoulders the coffin, covered with richly embroidered funeral cloth. The mausoleum has a romantic character, typical of the time and of its author, Arturo Mélida.

**Clock**. This huge artefact, performed by Friar José Cordero, hangs, in a neo-Classical box, above the gate.

**St. Christopher**. On the right-hand wall, there is an immense **fresco** of this *Saint protector of the travellers,* a work of the Italian artist known as Mateo Pérez de Alesio, who had worked in the Sistine Chapel; his signature is written in the peculiar parrot that is situated at the right lower part of the picture (1584). Its enormous dimensions, perfectly proportioned, do not affect the beauty of the drawing and the colour.

**Stained-glass windows** of this wing of the crossing. Above the door a rose window and *The Assumption* (31) (A. de Vergara, 1536); at the right-hand side: *St. Hermenegild, St. Jerome and St. Eustaquio* (32) (Maumejean, 1929-1932); across *St. Nicholas, St. Martin, St. Silvester and The Passing of The Virgin* (33); above the first nave, on the left-hand: *Doctors of the Latin Church* (34); on the right-hand side: *The Saints Justa, Rufina, Barbara and Catalina*(35) and opposite, the *Saints Inés, Lucia, and Cecilia* (37) (Arnao de Flandes, 1544-1556).

**Chapel of los Dolores**. Modern **stained-glass window** (38) in a chapel dedicated to *The Passion*. In the **altarpiece**, a *Crucified* (XVIth century); above the altar there is a dressed **image** of *The Vir-*

Christopher Columbus' funerary monument.

Altarpiece of the Chapel of Los Dolores.

Virgin of Los Dolores.

Sacristy of The Chalices.

Triangular candelabrum.

gin of *Los Dolores* (Pedro de Mena, 1680) and **paintings** with subjects of the Passion; across the altar, an *Ecce Homo*. *The Betrothal of The Virgin to St. Joseph* (Valdés Leal, 1657) and *Jacob blessing his children* (Pieter van Lint, XVIIth century) stand out among the pictures. The **mausoleum** of the Beatified Cardinal Spínola y Maestre, Canon and Archbishop of Seville (1896-1906), is erected in the front. A work of Joaquín Bilbao, it shows said Beatified in a praying position.

The magnificent and curious **Tenebrario** or Candelabrum that is used for the Holy Week cults: "The best devised, graceful and carried out piece of this genre in Spain". (Ceán Bermúdez). Hernán Ruíz designed it (1559), measures 7,8 mts. and is made of bronze (pedestal and rod) and of wood (the figures that crown it).

Above the chapel there is a stained-glass window (39): *Jesus washing the Apostles' feet* (Arnao de Flandes, 1555).

This chapel leads to the **Sacristy of the Chalices.** A wonder of soberness and proportion. It has rectangular ground plan (13,7 x 7,8 mts), and is one of the best achieved rooms of the architectural bridge between Gothic and Renaissance styles. It is formed by one square and two rectangular sections with stonework on the walls. Vaults are of Gothic ribs; at the corners the arches transform in squinches. The most distinguished architects of that century worked on this sacristy from 1509 to 1537: Alonso Rodríguez, Juan Gil de Hontañón, Diego de Riaño and Martín de Gainza. Two oratories are located at the far end. Noble and plain coffer, it contains a selection of immortal works of art.

*Sts. Justa and Rufina*, painting commissioned by the Chapter to Goya for this place. The halo around the heads of the saints comes from the right-hand window; the Guadalquivir River, the Cathedral and the Giralda are in the background; the two young ladies, with country-look faces, gaze at the sky. They carry bowls on their hands, as a reminder of their pottery craft, and the palms of martyrdom; rests of an idol are spread at their feet. A lion is licking Santa Rufina's feet. It is one of the most perfect religious works of the immortal painter from Aragón, who performed it in Seville in 1871.

The other **paintings** are likewise important: a *Crucified Christ* above the entrance; at the right-hand side, *Saint Ann, The Virgin and The Child* (Juan Bautista Caracciolo, XVIth century); *St. John The Baptist* (Zurbarán, 1640), *St. Peter freed by an Angel* (Valdés Leal,

Sts. Justa and Rufina.

Pietá accompanied by St. Vincent and St.Jerome, by Juan Núñez.

Mary between St. Peter and St. Jerome, by Juan Sánchez de Castro.

Lazarus with Martha and Mary,
by Juan Valdés Leal.

St. Peter liberated by an angel,
by Juan Valdés Leal.

1656), *The Holy Trinity* (Luis Tristán 1624), *The Calvary of the Donor* (Juan Sánchez II, XVth century), *The Epiphany* (Jordaens, 1669), *The Glory* (J. de Roelas, 1615), *The Virgin of the Rosary* (Zurbarán's School, XVIIth century), *The Guardian Angel* (Mattia Preti, 1660), *The Pietá, St. Vincent, St. Michael and Donor* (Juan Núñez, 1480), *The Circumcision of Jesus* (Jacobo Jordaens, 1669), *Lazarus with Martha and Mary* (Valdés Leal, 1658), *St. Jerome* (Legot, 1640); *Saints Justa and Rufina.* Left side: *St. Peter* (Pedro Fernández de Guadalupe, 1528), a tryptic by Alejo Fernádez: *The Birth of the Virgin* (1508), *Jesus Child is presented in the Temple* (1500) and *The Embrace of St. Joachim and St. Ann* (1508) and *The Adoration of the Magi* (1508); *The Virgin between St. Peter and St. Jerome* (J. Sánchez de Castro, XVth century). In the two chapels at the back two ivory crucifixes are exhibited, an image of the Virgin and several **trays**: in that of the left-hand side, *The Fuente de Paiva* of gilded silver, embossed and chiselled on both sides (XVth century), and another of Cardinal Delgado y Venegas (XVIIIth century). The showcases keep **chalices**, some of them of gold and precious stones, and a fretwork cup *The Reliquary of San Millán*, (Mexico, XVIth century).

**Chapel of St. Andrew.** Under a red canopy the figure of *The Holy Christ of Mercy* is erected, one of the most beautiful **sculptures** in the world and the most perfect of the Baroque crucifieds. It is the most important work of Martínez Montañés and an image of august grandness in which religiosity and art do blend: a perfect body, clean of blood, with just the necessary traces of the Passion. A shroud, placed with love, covers his nudity. It is an image of Jesus' mercy: his eyes are not of a judge, but of a saviour.

*Virgen del "Buen Aire"*. (Fair Wind) Patron saint of shipbuilders, captains and pilots of the Carrera de Indias (Indies Run) and

Dome of the Main Sacristy.

Mother of so many priests and seminarists that have been brought up at Her feet. Juan de Oviedo El Mozo performed it as a high-relief (1600) and Pedro Duque Cornejo transformed it in **ronde-bosse**, adding to it the wimple, the cloak, the seven angels base and the clouds; the crowns, the half-moon and the caravel were made by the goldsmith Juan de Garay (1721-1725). Some good **pictures** ornament the chapel. Four Gothic **sepulchres** of marble with reclining statues of three knights and a lady from the Pérez de Guzmán y Ayala family, the oldest of this chapel (XIVth-XVth century), coming from the temple-mosque, are leaned against the walls and the rails of the iron screens.

Above this chapel, a **stained-glass window** with *the Last Supper* (40) of Arnao de Flandes, 1555.

**Main Sacristy and Chapter House.** Behind the magnificent wrought-iron gate, a vestibule where one of the enormous choral books is exhibited. The Cathedral has more than three-hundred, illuminated by the best miniaturists of that time (XVth-XVIIIth century). *St. Anthony* (by Zurbarán or his School) is shown on the left-hand wall. Two large wooden cupboards with carved reliefs depicting Biblical scenes and female figures (Duque Cornejo, 1743) are almost covering the place.

This sacristy means something more than the space used by the celebrants to put on their vestments: it is an actual church with its altar and presbytery inside the Cathedral. Riaño (1528) began its

Cupola, exterior of the dome of the Main Sacristy.

43

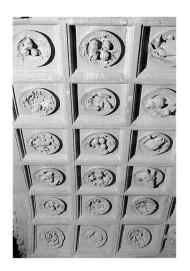

SOUTHERN CHAPELS

Dishes with food in the arch of access to the Main Sacristy.

Main Sacristy.

.St. Teresa, by Zurbarán.

construction and it was finished by Gaínza (1547). The doors are two works of art with **reliefs** of *St.Isidoro and St. Leandro* and *the Saints Justa and Rufina* and four medallions showing *The Evangelists;* on the back side, *heads of prophets, virtues and cherubim* displayed in hexagons (Diego Guillén Ferrant, 1548-1549). The Plateresque portal has its oblique arch adorned with caissons depicting several kind of foods: the menus of that time. The ground plan, a Greek cross, is roofed with a dome, measuring 18 mts long and 33 mts high. The pillars with carved pilasters that end in an ornamental frieze are erected over a podium; above, three sections of reliefs on different stages, that in the way of a catechist, enlighten about man's destiny: in the lower section The damned, and above them *Christ as Judge,* accompanied by *The Virgin, St John the Baptist and the Heavenly Court; The Trinity* in the lantern, the supreme saviour reality, while in the vaults are the blessed adoring.

Three altars, with the presbytery, are located at the head; in the vault of the central altar there is a **relief** of *The Assumption,* while the others are covered by caissons. These altars frame three unique paintings: *The Descent of Christ* from the Cross, by Pedro de Campaña (1547), oil painting on wood, dramatic in its composition and in the depicted characters. According to tradition, when Murillo contemplated it he was so captivated that, when he was told that it was time to leave, he used to say: "Let's wait until they finish descending Him". In the two other altars, Zurbarán's *St. Teresa de*

*Jesús* and *The Martyrdom of St. Lawrence* by Lucas Jordán: two unsurpassable pieces of work. These altars kept the relics until the XIXth century; nowadays they are used to show an ivory crucifix, two silver lecterns, effigies of Jesus Child, cherubim, paxes, pyxes, crosses; *The Head of St. John the Baptist,* made of polychrome wood by Juan de Mesa (1625) is specially outstanding; the tray is made of silver with enamels (XVIIIth century).

In the clean architecture of the lateral walls, other first class **pictorial works** are displayed: *St. Leandro* in symmetry with *St. Isidoro*: Murillo was commissioned by the Chapter to give splendour to this sacristy (1655). St. Isidoro lost in thoughts is reading while St. Leandro shows a sheet that says: "Believe, Goths, that He is inseparable from the Father", alluding to the Arian heresy against which he fought so bravely. The remaining pictures are *The Pietá* (Francisco Bayeu, 1788), *Sts. Justa and Rufina* (Miguel de Esquivel, 1620), *Vision of St. Francis in the Porcíncula* (Juan Sánchez Cotán, 1620), *Christ appearing to St. Ignatius* (Alonso Vázquez, 1595) and *The Virgin of La Merced* (Juan de Roelas, 1621).

Numerous jewels of this church are exhibited in this space.

In the middle of it, there is a huge **Monstrance** carried out by Juan de Arfe y Villafañe (1580-1587) who considered it as "the largest and best silver piece known of this kind". It measures 3,90 mts. and weighs almost 475 kgs. It consists of four sections of twenty-four columns each one. It encloses a whole doctrine about the Eucharist: in the first section, of Ionic order, the militant Church represented in thirty-six Biblical scenes and six images of Saints that surround The Immaculate (initially it was the Faith; the Virgin and the six lily vases were added later on; Juan Segura, 1668); the second section, Corinthian, that praises the Eucharist, foreshadowed in six bas-reliefs with sacrifices from the Old Testament; in the middle, the monstrance, holding the Bread of Life, surrounded by saints of popular tradition; the third, of Composite order, symbolizes the triumphant Church around the Lamb of the Apocalypse, with medaillons alluding to Jesus' Sacrifice, fringed by statues of saints; and in the last one, of Composite order, The Holy Trinity, origin and destiny of all salvation, which culmination is Faith, that arises up on top with the Christian standard. The minor adorns also have an Eucharistic meaning: children, birds, vine leaves. This iconographic program was carried out by the Canon Francisco Pacheco. The skirts are from the XVIIIth century and are embroidered with silk and silver.

.Processional Custodian by Juan de Arfe.

*Processional image of St.. Ferdinand.* Pedro Roldán, a sculptor from Seville, performed it commissioned by the Chapter at the time the Saintly King was canonized (1671). The processional base is made of silver. It goes in procession on Corpus Christi day.

*Processional image of the Immaculate* also called the "Tiny Conception", work of the Sevillian sculptor Alonso Martínez (1658). It goes in procession on the same festivity.

*The Giants*, two of the four candelabrums, called that way due to their height; they are made of embossed and chiselled silver (Hernando de Ballesteros el Mozo, 1579-1581).

**First Showcase.** Six couples of silver **Reliquaries** (Francisco de Alfaro, 1600).*Reliquary of St. Christopher*, of gilded silver, its upper part being of an hexagonal shape (XIVth century), while the lower is of the XVIIth century. **The Santo Lignum Crucis**, of cross shape, is made of gold, precious stones, enamels and splendid cameos. A Pietá and five gold statuettes form its base and in its hollowed out foot there are carved subjects of the Resurrection and the Donor's coat of arms; another curious reliquary, that of St. Clement, also called the "Coco" because of its shape (both of the XIVth century).

**Second Showcase.** *Jars for the Holy Oils* made of gilded and embossed silver (Antwerp, 1564). Aguamanil de la Sierpe of gilded, embossed and chiselled silver; its spout depicts a snake, its handle is an enamelled lizard and the cover a dragon with the world globe; a Portuguese work (XVth century). *The purple pall,* the *white dalmatic* and *the alb with lace* are samples of the cathedral trousseau composed of more than 3.000 cloth pieces: capes, chasubles, dalmatics, etc.

**Third Showcase.** *Tablas Alfonsinas.* Romanic tryptic of larch wood covered with gilded silver, gold adorns, and encrusted precious stones, enamels and cameos. In the front side, caissons with relics covered with rock crystal; in the back side, heraldic medaillons and reliefs of *The Annunciation* and *The Epiphany.* It weighs over 18 kgs. and is attributed to the silversmith Juan de Toledo; it was donated by Alphonso X The Wise (1284). It is one of the most curious and interesting jewels of the Spanish Gothic silver work.

*City Keys.* According to tradition, King Axafat handed them to St. Ferdinand: The smallest one is made of wrought iron with Arabic inscriptions; the other key, made of silver, has inscriptions in rabbinical hebrew and monastic characters.

**Fourth Showcase**. *Pectoral Cross of Clement the XIVth with Lignum Crucis.* The Chapter framed the present of the Pope in this

St. Ferdinand, by Pedro Roldán.

Tablas Alfonsíes.

47

Patio of The Óleos.

extremely rich reliquary of solid gold; a globe map (XVIIIth century) is chiselled in the world globe. *Pectoral Cross, Pin and Diamonds Ring,* a present of Isabel the IInd to Cardinal Tarancón (XIXth century); also several other pectoral crosses and episcopal rings; *Four reliquary coffers* by Hernando de Ballesteros El Viejo (1559); Manuel Guerrero (1730-1740) performed the other two.

**Patio of The Óleos**. Square room, in the open, it is a work of Diego de Riaño and Martín de Gainza (1529-1537) and is composed of three plants: a series of arches on columns form galleries with balustrades in three of their sides; the fourth one corresponds to the wall of the façade. An artistic vertical position characterizes it since the only point of light is the empty space of the patio.

**Patio of the Chapter or of El Mariscal.** Ideal solution of Hernán Ruíz's architecture: a square space, in the open air; its sides are adorned with doors and windows, some of them are simulated, and its pediments with heads (one might depict the author). Above, there is an iron balustrade (1560-1570). Joined on to, in the *Sala de las Columnas* three processional crosses are exhibited: The *Merino Cross,* in Renaissance style, of gilded silver with gold enamels, cameos and jaspe (Francisco Merino, 1587); The *white crystal Cross*, made of golden silver, rock crystal and red and green jaspe (Hernando de Ballesteros, XVIth century); the third one is of gilded silver.

Above the Main Sacristy, **Stained-Glass Window** (41) by Arnao de Flandes (1556): *The Cleansing of the Temple.*

Ante-Chapter-House.

**Ante-Chapter-House**. Entering through the chapel of The Mariscal, can be admired, from a kind of small vestibule, the stone and jade portal, that ends in a semicircular arch and a skylight, with two doors: on the left, a relief of Solomon (medallion) and Jesus (rectangle); on the right, *David and The Virgin Mary*. The Ante-Chapter, an architectonic wonder, was built by Hernán Ruíz and Asensio de Maeda (1560-1582). It has a rectangular ground plan (12x6 mts.), a caissoned vault ending in a square lantern, four doors in perfect symmetry and one more of access to the Chapter-House; its flooring is of white and black marble. A continuous stone seat surrounds it. The ornamentation, on a reliefs basis, is very soigné: on the door tympanums The *Four Evangelists* and

*Noah and the Flood;* on the side walls that are separated by marble pilasters, *Ten Episodes of the Bible and Allegories* and eight figures of *The Virtues:* everything of marble. The decoration is of Diego de Pesquera (1575-1580) and the inscriptions by the Canon Francisco Pacheco. Ceán Bermúdez commented about this room:"The Ante-Chapter-House could appropriately be used as Chapter House for the first cathedrals in Spain, due to its capacity, for its good shape and for the magnificence of its decoration".

**Chapter-House.** A curved passage leads to one of the most admirable areas of the Spanish Renaissance architecture. The door, of jasper, is adorned on its inner part with pilasters and doric façade, adorned with small figures of children (putti). Its elliptical ground plan measures on its largest axis 14 mts. and 9 mts. on the smallest one; Hernán Ruíz designed and began it (1558) and Asensio de Maeda finished it (1592). The flooring with the same drawing that Michelangelo contrived for the square of the Rome Capitol is impressing. The space is divided into clearly defined areas: the lower plan or of the seats is presided by the *Archbishop's Chair*, made of inlaid mahogany and ornamented with three small sculptures; in front is the Secretary's bench (Diego Velasco, 1529) and a pad dressed stone seat surrounds it. A doric cornice held by angels runs over it, and above a panelling decorated by eight allegoric paintings with inscriptions, and, among them, *Giraldas and lily vases*, the coat of arms of this Cathedral and of its Chapter (Pablo de Céspedes, 1529). The second section, of Ionic order, is divided by half-columns that frame the **high-relief**s: the larger eight have as subjects: *The Assumption of The Virgin,* (in the front); *The Smoke from the Hell and Christ, The Witness arising from the Candelabrums, The Cleansing of the Temple and The Allegory of the Last Judgement* displayed at the sides; *The Mystic Lamb* is above the door and at their sides *Angels with Clarion and Angel with legs like fire columns.* They were carried out by Juan Bautista, Vázquez el Viejo, Diego de Pesquera and Diego de Velasco (1582-1584). The small **reliefs** show the following subjects, starting with *The Assumption, The Last Sermon of Jesus, Daniel among the lions receiving food from Habacuc, Storm in the Tiberiades, The Sower, The Agony in the Garden, St. Peter's Vision, Christ washing the Feet of The Apostles* (Marcos Cabrera). Diverse Latin inscriptions with golden letters on dark marble (Francisco Pacheco) alternate with the reliefs. From the cornice of this section springs a vault with caissons, divided in three concentric ellipses, with seven circular windows (oculus) that, along

Chapter House.

Vault of the Chapter-House.

Detail of the Chapter-House flooring.

with the lantern, allow the passing of light. The vault is an anthology of Murillo's **paintings** (1677). The Immaculate, one of his most beautiful images presides it; in circular format there are eight saints (considered) to be from Seville: *St. Hermenegild, St. Ferdinand, St. Leandro, St. Isidoro, St. Laureano, St. Justa, St. Rufina and St. Pío.* The Chapter coat of arms (Pedro de Medina Valbuena, 1668) appears in the remaining space of the vault. It ends in an elliptical lantern over Corinthian columns. The Chapter's task is shown in a cartouche at the entrance: *To provide choir and altar.*

**Former Counting-House**. It is called that way inasmuch it used to be the financial management. The same Ante-Chapter vestibule leads to it. Its portal is lintel-like with attic (Hernán Ruíz, 1560); its ground plan is rectangular (11 x 7 mts.), and it is roofed with a coffered ceiling with golden caissons and pine-cones. It is used to exhibit numerous jewels of the Cathedral. In the middle, The **Tiny Monstrance** or *Monstrance of the Saint Thorn*; a piece of embossed and chiselled silver of Renaissance style (Francisco de Alfaro, 1600). It files by on procession on the Corpus Christi day. *Scale-model of* **The Large Monstrance**: wooden model that Juan de Arfe presented to the Chapter on 1580.

At the right-hand side of the entrance. **First Showcase.** *Precious Monstrance,* made of gold, diamonds, two thick pearls, emeralds and rubies; a Sevillian work by Ignacio Thamaral (1729). *Large Monstrance*, of gilded silver, emeralds, diamonds and fifteen hundred pearls in bunches; Italian Baroque (1778).

**Second Showcase.** *Urn for the Maundy Thursday Pyx*, of gold and gilded silver (Luis Valadier, 1771); *two keys with gold chains for the urn* (1807). *Censer and gold container for incense* (Antonio Méndez, 1791). *Gold cruet stands,* from Mexico. Embossed silver *Tray.*

**Third Showcase.** *Two amphoras, a jar* and *a tray* of embossed silver.

**Fourth Showcase.** *Gothic cross and Alfonsíe candlesticks,* of gilded, embossed and chiselled silver (1486-1502). **Pax** shaped like a small altarpiece, of gold and precious stones with the Virgin of enamel. (XVIth century).

A beautiful **image** of *St. Joseph* of carved and polychrome wood by Pedro Roldán (1664), presides over the parlour.

**Fifth Showcase.** *Crowns of the Virgin of the Kings and Jesus Child* in gold, pearls, diamonds, and precious stones, made in Seville for the canonical crowning. Tray of golden and embossed silver.

**Sixth Showcase.** *Cross-reliquary* of gold, enamels and precious stones. Couple of Paxes with the Ascension and the Assumption, of chiselled and gilded silver. (Ballesteros el Viejo, 1556). Pax of St. Ann made of golden and chiselled silver, (XVIth century). Pax in shape of a small temple: The Virgin with The Child in the middle and Philip the Vth of France and Jeanne of Burgundy (Paris, about 1320) in the doors. Platter-*tray with coat of arms of the Chapter* of golden silver (Vicente Gargallo, 1700).

**Seventh Showcase.** *Altar cross*, made of silver (XVth century). *Cross-reliquary of the Lignum-Crucis* (XVIth century). *Reliquary of St. Clement:* Chalice of gold the cup of which is a large agatha over which a gold made St. Clement appears (1516).

**Eighth Showcase.** *Two cups with their dishes,* of chiselled gold (Mexico, XVIIIth century). *Pyx of Maundy Thursday*, of gold, diamonds, emeralds and rubies (XVIIIth century). *Tray* of embossed and chiselled silver with golden adorns and coat of arms (1778). Chalice made of gold and diamonds.

**Bust** of *St. Rosalía* of embossed and chiselled silver; it weighs 42,250 kgs. (Antonio L. Castelli, Palermo 1681). Donation of Archbishop Palafox in 1688.

.Exterior of the former Counting-House.

St. Joseph, by Pedro Roldán.

Pax of Philippe V of France.

**Chapel of El Mariscal.** "One of the most distinguished jewels that dignify the temple" (Gestoso). Classicism and beauty everywhere. If the iron gate depicting *The Holy Burial* is beautiful (M. de Gainza and Pedro Delgado, 1555), the stained-glass window *The Betrothal of the Virgin and St. Joseph* (Arnao de Flandes, 1556) is not inferior; it emphasizes the beauty of the altarpiece of paintings (1555-1556); in the central painting *The Purification of The Virgin,* a masterpiece of the Spanish Renaissance, although its author, Pedro de Campaña, was Peter Kampeneer, a Flemish artist who worked in this temple. The composition is perfect and the female faces, that evoke those of Rafael Sanzio, matchless; vestments and colour add beauty to the whole. Other equally beautiful works of art are in the altar plan: *Jesus Child among the Doctors* and at their sides groups of *portraits of the Donor and his family,* of clear Flemish inspiration; other paintings are Vision of *St. Ildefonsus, St. James, St. Dominic and St. Francis,* with the appearance of Michelangelo's prophets in the Sistine Chapel. A *Resurrection* and above it a *Calvary* are in the attic. Don Diego Caballero, marshal (mariscal) of the Island of La Española, the name is after it, commissioned it to Pedro de Campaña.

### EASTERN CHAPELS

A painting of *St. Roque* (A. de Alfián) hangs in the interior, at both sides of the door.

**Altar of The Tutelary Saints**. Very Sevillian group of *Saints Justa and Rufina with the Giralda* (Duque Cornejo, 1728): two pretty girls seem to hold, caress and protect the City symbol. It goes out on procession on Corpus Christi day.

**Altar of St. Barbara**. Altarpiece with ten interesting paintings by Antonio Rodríguez (1545): *The Holy Family with an angel that offers some grapes to The Child,* over it *Whitsuntide* and on the sides several saints, among them *St. Barbara.* An image of *St. Anthony* calls this chapel St. Antonio Chico.

Above the portal of the Campanilla, a **stained-glass window** of *St. Christopher* (42) (Arnao de Flandes, 1546).

**Chapel of The Immaculate of Grande.** St. Paul was its incumbent as the interior **stained-glass window** depicting *The Conversion of St. Paul* (Arnao de Flandes, 1550) does testify. The magnificent altarpiece, of Solomonic order (Francisco Dionisio de Ribas y Martín Moreno, XVIIth century), shows in its centre a

beautiful sculpture of *The Immaculate*, in polychrome wood, accompanied by *St. Joseph, St. Paul, St. Gonzalo and St. Anthony of Padua*. The *Crucifix* belonged to the former chapel (XVIth century). Above *God Father* surrounded by the virtues and angels; the sculptures are from Alonso Martínez. A marble slab on the left-hand side evokes the Sepúlveda family that dedicated the chapel to the Immaculate; the coat of arms of this family is shown in the iron screen (1654). On the right-hand wall, there is the *sepulchre of Cardinal Don Francisco J. Cienfuegos y Jovellanos* (1824-1847); the tumulus with the reclining statue of the deceased dressed with his pontifical vestments is over a base; it is ornamented with figures of the Virtues, angels and his coat of arms (Manuel Portillo, 1881). The name of *The Immaculate Grande* serves to distinguish it from *The Immaculate Chica*, located in the Main Sacristy.

**Royal Chapel: Marian Sanctuary of the City of Mary.** The remains of St. Ferdinand, his wife Doña Beatriz de Suavia, his son Alfonso X The Wise and other royal dignitaries lay in this place of the mosque-cathedral. The fact of being a Royal Pantheon

Chapel of El Mariscal. Detail.

The Patron Saints Justa and Rufina.

EASTERN CHAPELS

55

.Royal Chapel.

conditioned its history: the move of the royal bodies was not allowed until 1433, with King Juan the IInd, making possible its construction. Martín de Gainza designed and started it (1541), Hernán Ruíz continued with the work and Juan de Maeda finished it. The report from the Chapter to the King Felipe the IInd is dated on July 19, 1575. The bodies were moved on June 13, 1579.

The splendid **iron screen** (Sebastián van der Borcht, 1755), donated by Carlos the IIIrd (1771), shows on its top a sculpture of St. Ferdinand receiving the Keys of the City, made of wood covered with

Virgin of The Kings.

lead (Jerónimo Roldán). The chapel, that seeks to evoke the Saint Sepulchre of Jerusalem and the Pantheon of Rome, is square shaped with a semicircular apse. Eight adorned **pilasters** form seven spaces: *The Throne of the Virgin* accompanied by *St. Peter and St. Paul and The Four Evangelists*, below *St. Isidoro and St. Leandro, Sts. Justa and Rufina*; two chapels with tribunes which arches show medallions with the *heads of Garci and Diego Pérez de Vargas*, companions of St. Ferdinand; in the last ones, the Royal Sepulchres. A frieze depicting children with lances and alberds runs around it. Its ceiling is a dome of caissons with heads of kings in relief that culminates in a lantern. *The twelve kings of Judea* (entrance arch) and a *theory of sculptures* that seem to look for the zenith as if an inner force stimulate them (apse) stand out in the ornamentation. The images of Pedro de Campaña and Diego de Pesquera were carried out by Pedro Campos and Lorenzo de Bao (1571-1574). The Lady of Seville, The *Virgin of the Kings* is shown seated on Her throne (1806) with Her Child on Her knees and under a silver baldachin *(Per me reges regnant (Kings reign thanks to me)*; they measure 1,76 and 0,64 mts. These images can be clothed, with articulated arms and hands, of carved and polychrome larch wood in the visible parts. Belonging to the transitional period between Romanic and Gothic styles, the Virgin reflects the majesty of a Queen, although without any hieratic attitude, and the Child shows an amazing naturalness in his innocent face, his cunning smile and his curled hair. Tradition considers it as a property of St. Ferdinand who donated it to the Cathedral. It has always presided this chapel and it was canonically crowned on December 4, 1904. A **relief** of *Isaiah's Vision* is above the altar and above it *The Heavenly Father*. The altar antependium and the side-tables are made of silver (Villaviciosa, 1739) and the candelabrums with two-head eagles come from Peru.

**The Sepulchral Urn** contains St. Ferdinand's remains, recently buried, cleaned and reconstructed. The body is dressed with royal vestments carrying on his hands the baton and a sword. The urn (Juan Laureano de Pina, 1655-1719), donated by Felipe the IInd, lies over a marble pedestal from the original sepulchre at which sides the eulogy in Arabic, Hebrew, Latin and Spanish that Alfonso the Xth made of his father: "The most loyal, the most truthful, the most frank, the most vigorous, the most handsome, the most distinguished, the most sufferer, the most modest, the one who most feared God and most served Him (...), and conquered the city of Seville that is head of all Spain...".

The free-standing altar shows a silver antependia carried out by the Sevillians Resiente and Villaviciosa, contemporaneous of the urn. A small crypt is under the sepulchre where the remains of other royal persons are laying at rest and *The Virgin of the Battles,* a **seated image** (XIIIth century) that accompanied St. Ferdinand in his campaigns.

The monumental *sepulchres of Alfonso X the Wise and of his mother Doña Beatriz de Suavia* are placed in large Renaissance niches (XVIth century). Both figures, in praying position, look at the altar, the faces are made of alabaster and the rest is of marble. They were carried out by Antonio Cano Correa and his wife (that of the King) and Juan Luis Vasallo Parodi (the Queen), in the celebration

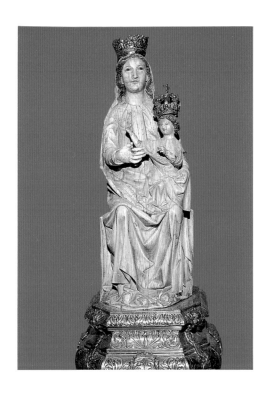

Virgin of The Battles.

Dome of the Royal Chapel.

of the seventh centennial of the conquest of Seville. Two holy water stoups engraved with a very good taste are at the chapel entrance (XVIIIth century). In the lateral chapels is the choir of the royal chaplains, the sacristy and a small museum dedicated to St. Ferdinand.

Above the Royal Chapel two **stained-glass windows**: *The Evangelists* (44) (1547) and *Jesus with the Cross* (45) (1535) by Arnao de Flandes.

**Chapel of St. Peter.** Framed in an altarpiece of utmost plainness (XVIIth century) an incomparable **painting** collection of Zurbarán in the Incumbent's honour, is exhibited: *St. Peter, The Pope* and on their sides *Vision of the impure animals and Repentance*; above, the insuperable *Immaculate Conception*, flanked by the *Quo Vadis?* (Where are you going?) and *St. Peter's release*; three scenes more, above the altar: *St. Peter walking on the Water, Delivery of the Keys* and *The Cure of the Paralytic*; on top, *The Heavenly Father* (copy). The two stained-glass windows allude to the *Incumbent*: above the altarpiece *St. Peter Bishop* (Arnao de Flandes, XVIth century) and on the left-hand side, *Papal Emblems* (1784), that also stand in the iron screen (Friar José Cordero, 1780). This small museum includes also other paintings with subjects of the Order of La Merced, by Juan Luís Zambrano and two others with topics of St. Peter's life. *The Sepulchre of archbishop Friar Diego de Deza* (1504-1523) is placed on the left side: under an arch the prelate figure with pontifical vestments lies with a lion at his feet. It dates from a few years after his death and it comes from Santo Tomás' College. The *Almohad doorknockers* of the Forgiveness Gate are here exhibited.

**Door of Palos**. It is worthwhile to emphasize the extreme beauty and more than curious **stained-glass window** (46) in which *St. Sebastian* appears as Carlos the Vth with his emblems (A. de Vergara, 1535); a painting of the same Saint (Antonio Alfián, XVIth century) is above the door.

**Altar of The Assumption.** On both sides of the door, a subject depicted in relief in the centre, with *St. Ildefonse and St. Diego de Alcalá.* (Alonso Vázquez, 1539).

**Altar of The Magdalene.** In this altarpiece of nine paintings on panel, of Alejo Fernández School (XVIth century) *The apparition of Jesus to Mary Magdalene* and the *Donors* stand out, and in the second section *The Annunciation to Mary.*

In the retrochoir, two **stained-glass windows** of Arnao de Flandes: *The Evangelists* (47) (1547) and *Jesus with the Cross* (48) (1535).

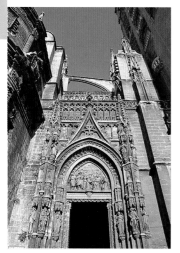

Door of Los Palos, from a different angle.

St. Peter by Zurbarán.

St. Peter dressed in
Pope's vestments.

St. Peter's confession by
Zurbarán.

Altarpiece of the Main Chapel.

## A CATHEDRAL INSIDE THE CATHEDRAL

**The Main Chapel** forms an open unit closed by a stonework wall with works and Gothic statues of baked clay and very good workmanship, and enormous iron screens (1522-1575). These walls were built successively by Miguel Florentín (from 1522), Juan Marín (1564) and Diego de Pesquera (1571). Eighteen statues are in the

The central iron screen
from the High Altar.

central area and sixteen on the laterals. The central area is presided (opposite to the Royal Chapel) by the gorgeous **image** of the *Virgin of the Repose with The Child*, that was of great devotion among the pregnant women of Seville. It measures 1,53 mts.; a work of Miguel Perrín (1540). At one side of the Virgin there are three statues and four at the other side, "because the Gothic architects did not care about the eurhythmy" (Ceán Bermúdez).

View of the transept.

**Iron Screens.** Three Renaissance gilded wrought iron screens close off the presbytery without blocking it up. The central one, designed by Bartolomé de Jaén and carried out by Friar Francisco de Salamanca (1524-1528), is articulated on six corinthian columns over pedestals and embellished with reliefs. The centre of the first frieze, with fretted decoration and angels, has as the centre a **medallion** with the face of *The Saviour*; in the second *Five Prophets* and above

an iron picture depicting *The Burial of Jesus* flanked by candela-brums, flames and little angels, and above them the Cross. On the sides, two pulpits raise over iron columns and marble pedestals, work of the same artists. The two lateral iron screens are more an-cient: over Gothic bases the pilasters rise ending in fretted friezes with flames and candelabrums (Sancho Muñoz and Diego de Huido-bro, 1518-1523). Two colossal silver lamps hang next to these iron screens.

The "Seises" before the High Altar.

**Altarpiece: And, at the front side, in the background, the golden and vertical area and collection of a universe of fig-ures, display of orderly fantasy, immense altarpiece (Manuel Ferrand).**

In spite of not appearing in the Guiness Book, it is the largest area of **polychrome woodwork** that exists: 18,20 mts wide by 27,80 mts high. It is shaped like a tryptic for giants, topped by a canopy-dust-cover and crowned by an upper section (beam) and dominating everything a unique Calvary. The Flemish Pyeter Dancart designed and started it (1481-1488), his followers were Master Marco, Pedro Millán, the brothers Jorge and Alejo Fernández, sculptor and painter; Roque de Balduque and Juan Bautista Vázquez

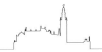

Scale model of Seville, in the altarpiece.

the Elder. It was finished on January 17, 1526. The laterals were carried out later on (1549-1564). Of Gothic style, it is carved in walnut, laburnum and chestnut wood. The central panel is articulated in seven vertical sections and five horizontal ones, the lower part being smaller. In this mentioned section three sculptural groups with views of Seville are outstanding. In the **central section** the following can be admired, from the bottom on: *Birth, Assumption, Resurrection and Ascension*. The remaining pictures follow a horizontal sequence, starting from the lower right, with a catechise about Jesus' life. New scenes about the Saviour's life appear on the sides, mixed with others taken also from the Bible: forty four reliefs in all. In the pilasters one hundred eighty nine small sculptures alternate, some of them are very beautiful. The huge **canopy** is formed by caissons and crowned by an *Apostolate* and on its centre *The Fifth Anguish:* Mary with Jesus' body and the Saintly Women (Jorge and Alejo Fernández). As a crown of this forest of polychrome wood, *The Christ of the Million*, a Crucified

flanked by the Virgin and St. John: "it is a masterly piece due to its drawing, modelling, carving, composition, polychromy and holy unction, that dramatizes the scholastic naturalism peculiar to the middle Gothic". (José Hernández Díaz). The origin of its name is not exactly known: perhaps due to the favours that He bestowed or for the indulgences obtained praying to Him. The perfection of all the figures is admirable, even the most remote ones; the adornments seem to be made by a miniaturist. The scenes of *The Creation* and *The Paradise* of Juan Bautista Vázquez The Elder (1561-1563) stand out at the laterals.

Epiphany, detail of the altarpiece.

**Virgin of The See**. In the centre of the lower section, the *Incumbent* of this church presides the altar. Seated image, Her face shines of beauty and on Her hand She holds a crystal apple garnished with silver; the Child blesses the world globe. Height work of the Spanish Medieval sculpture (XIIIth century), it is carved in cypress wood with polychrome embodiments while the remaining parts are covered with embossed and chiselled silver.

Virgin of the See.

Lectern in the High Altar.

A CATHEDRAL INSIDE
THE CATHEDRAL

According to tradition this image used to stay in St. Ferdinand's camp from where it went to preside the ceremonies that changed the large Mosque into a Christian Cathedral (Christmas 1248). The silver work is ascribed to Sancho Muñoz (1366).

**The Tabernacle.** The gilded and embossed silver Tabernacle is located on the altar, adorned with columns, reliefs and statuettes, and two huge lecterns, also made of silver (Francisco de Alfaro, 1593-1596). Two **sculptures** are exhibited in the upper presbytery of *St. Isidoro and St. Leandro:* faces and hands made of polychrome wood and their vestments silver-plated with inlaid precious stones (1741); they belong to the silver altar. There is also a peculiar *Lectern* shaped like an angel that holds, kneeling down and over his back, the book of readings, of polychrome and golden wood (Francisco A. Girón, XVIIth century): from the extraordinary choir used on Maundy Thursday and Corpus Christi day. In the lower presbytery stand up the large silver **candelabrums**, the so-called *Vizarrones,*

as they were donated by Archbishop and Viceroy of Mexico, Don Juan Antonio Vizarrón (1744).

Two **stained-glass windows** look on to the lower presbytery, *Death of the Virgin* (49) and *Glorification* (50) (Jean Jacques, 1511-1518).

**Chancel.** Space between the Choir and the High Chapel.

Above this space, four triple **stained-glass windows**, two of them by A. de Vergara *Presentation, Annunciation and Visitation* (51) (1525); *Looking for the Child, Jesus among the Doctors* and *The Encounter* (52) (1526); the remaining ones are modern (1913).

**Choir**. It occupies the space of the fourth and fifth vault and is situated in the central nave, close to the Main Chapel. Three of its sides are closed in by stonework walls and the fourth by a splendid golden **iron screen** and of Plateresque style the subject of which is The *Tree of Jese*, and from which lying body sprout the branches that culminate in Jesus. It tells about Christ' humanity. On its sides are situated medaillons with four apostles (Francisco de Salamanca,

Light and shade in the central naves.

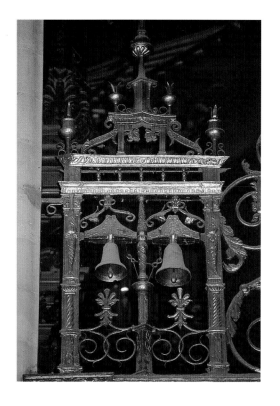

Small bells in the iron-screen of the Choir.

Iron screen of the Choir, detail.

1518-1523). The space of the choir measures 20 x 14 mts. The choir-stalls are a jewel in its genre with one hundred and seventeen seats: sixty seven in the upper part and fifty in the lower one. Gothic-Mudejar, it is made of precious woods. The lower choir-stalls show on the seats the Giralda of that time, in marquetry; on the heads scenes from the Bible in relief and in the misericordes (front part of the movable section of the seats) monstrous representations of vices and sins. The upper choir-stalls are similar; however above the seats rise up arches sustained by one hundred and fourteen small wooden statues and, above the arches, a canopy of cresting supported by seventy two small figures. The Archbishop's seat and prie-dieu and the chairs of his assistants are specially beautiful; they are ascribed to master Guillén, author of the Main Sacristy doors (1548). In the King's ceremonial chair, the second on the left-hand side facing the altar, the coat of arms of Castile and León of marquetry and the inscription: "Nufro Sánchez, engraver, that in

The Virgin in the lectern top.

.St. Joseph in the choir stalls.

God be, built this choir. It was finished in 1478" although it was finished by Pyeter Dancart.

**Lectern.** A huge lectern with four faces of wood and bronze that was also used for the likewise gigantic choir books. It turns over a round foot and it is adorned with medaillons of figures allusive to music (Juan Marín, Juan Bautista Vázquez the Elder and Francisco Hernández, sculptors, and the smelter Bartolomé Morel, 1562-1565). It culminates in a small temple with an image of the Virgin, a Crucifix and the Evangelists (Bautista Vázquez). The grandeur of this beautiful contrivance is not in conflict with the delicacy of its design and its finishing.

**Organs.** A monument to music and to the musicians that gave glory to this Cathedral. The masters Guerrero (1549-1599), Antonio de Ripa (1768-1795), Hilarión Eslava (1830-1847) and Eduardo Torres

Organ: side of the Epistle.

(1910-1934) among others should be mentioned. The construction of these organs began in 1724 and since then the mechanism has been modernized several times. They include two with double face and a single console. The outside, cases and cornices, are a work of Luis de Vilches (1724-1741) while the sculptures are by Duque Cornejo. Organs and music evoke as well those heavenly moments that are the dances of the Seises, that only this Cathedral has kept. Dur-

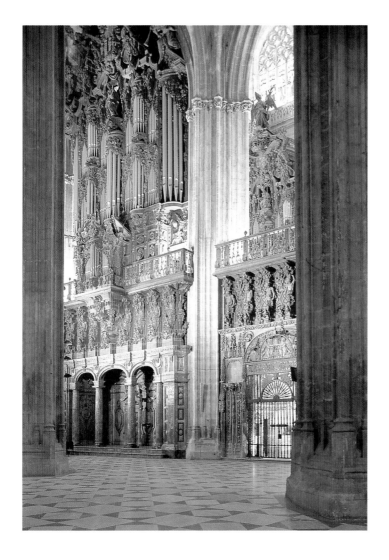

Organ: side of the Gospel and chapels of The Alabastros.

ing the eight days that follow the festivities of the Immaculate and the Corpus Christi, at five thirty p.m., ten children, dressed in page clothing, dance in front of the Blessed Sacrament, wearing hats and accompanied by castanets; dances and songs with a flavour of centuries, that calm our spirits and raise our hearts; the past becomes present in their music and dances.

Four **stained-glass windows** with four spaces look on to the

Vault roofing choir and organ.

choir: *Dignitaries from The Old Testament* (53) (A. de Vergara, 1535); *Kings and celebrities from Israel* (54) (E. Alemán, 1478-1483); *Major Prophets* (55) (Zettler, 1908).

**Porticos**. On each side of the choir there are elegant polychrome marble porticos (Diego Antonio Díaz, 1725), followed by the chapels of Los Alabastros, called thus for the material utilized on their construction.

Virgin of Genoa.

The filtered light is reflected in the retrochoir flooring.

**Lateral chapels**

At the *side of the Epistle* the chapels are of Juan Gil de Hontañón, 1518:

**Chapel of The Immaculate**. A small room with a series of the most important works of Montañés: *The Little Blind Girl,* a young Virgin, serene and inward-looking, that invites to pray; her downcast eyes have given her that popular name. She is accompanied by *St. John The Baptist Child* work of an unimaginable perfection, and *St. Gregory;* the **reliefs** of *St. Joseph, St. Joachim, St. Jerome and St. Francis* are also by Montañés. The portraits of the *Donors* and the polychromy of the images (1628-1631) were performed by Francisco Pacheco. Iron screen of the XVIIth century.

**Virgin of Genoa.** This image of the Virgin (73 cm) is located between this chapel and the next one, an Italian piece of polychrome alabaster that used to belong to an old brotherhood of Genoese people established in Seville (XIVth century).

**Chapel of The Encarnación**. Both *The Annunciation,* in the centre, as the half-length figures of *St. John The Baptist, St. John The Evangelist, St. Dominic, St. Francis and St. Anthony* belong to Montañés' School; on top, a relief of *The Heavenly Father* (1630-1635). The Baroque iron screen reminds the patrons.

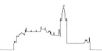

Retrochoir.

**Retrochoir.** This Cathedral is characterized by the spaciousness and brightness of this sector. It occupies one third of the temple length; it is illuminated by the stained-glass windows of the main nave, the second naves and of the chapels. Its altar takes up the whole wide of the main nave and it is about 8 mts. high. The elegant design, the jaspers of different colours, the bronzes, sculptures and paintings enhance the **painting** on wood of *The Virgin of the Remedios*, depicted with a saintly bishop and a kneeling priest (XIVth century), one of the oldest and most beautiful of this church. A bronze by Francisco Pacheco is exhibited beneath: *The surrender of Seville to St. Ferdinand* (1663), on the laterals there are four reliefs with eucharistic topics and above the wickets there are busts of *Saints Justa y Rufina*, in the attic sculptures with a child in the centre (XVIth century). It was designed by Miguel de Zumárraga and finished by Pedro Sánchez Falconete between 1620-1635.

The chapels on the *Gospel side* were built by Gil de Hontañón and Diego de Riaño, 1523-1532.

**Chapel of The Virgin of the Star**, a beautiful image that might have been carried out by the French artist Nicolás de León (1530; a polychromy of the XVIIIth century); at the sides, sculptures

Virgin of The Star.

St. Clement.

of *St. Joachim and St. Ann*. The screen is an iron embroidery, designed by Hernán Ruíz (1568).

**Chapel of St. Gregory**. The image of the Incumbent is in the centre, made of polychrome wood. The book that he carries in his hand shows the signature of its author, Manuel García de Santiago is shown (XVIIIth century). The ornamentation is Plateresque and the iron screen is of 1650.

**"This is the tent that God has built among men and God Himself will live with them"**
**(Apocalipsis. 21, 3)**

THE REPRINTING OF THIS BOOK, PUBLISHED BY ALDEASA, WAS

FINISHED ON THE 15TH OF NOVEMBER, 1996 AT

JULIO SOTO, IMPRESOR, S. A., MADRID